MAS HIERARCHY OF NEEDS

Gain vital insights into how to motivate people

Written by Pierre Pichère
In collaboration with Anne-Christine Cadiat
Translated by Carly Probert

Business   50MINUTES.com

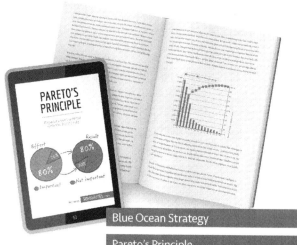

MASLOW'S HIERARCHY OF NEEDS

KEY INFORMATION

- **Name:** Maslow's Hierarchy of Needs, Maslow's Pyramid of Needs.
- **Uses:** psychology and social sciences (to categorise and prioritise individual needs), marketing and management.
- **Why is it successful?** It is a dynamic visual representation of needs, including both physiological and spiritual aspects.
- **Key words:** psychology, needs, Maslow, pyramid.

INTRODUCTION

Economic science is the allocation of limited resources according to the infinite needs, motivations and expectations of individuals. But how do you define needs? That is what this pyramid, developed by the American psychologist Abraham Harold Maslow (1908-1970), tries to do.

History

Starting in the 1940s, Maslow, along with Carl Rogers (psychologist, 1902-1987), introduced a new approach to humanistic psychology. In his works, Maslow studied the structure of human needs. His readers and supporters later formalised his theses in the form of a pyramid.

There are five levels of needs:

- physiological needs

- safety needs
- need for recognition
- need for esteem
- need for self-actualisation.

Each of these categories corresponds to human activities. This model has been widely used in economics and in the corporate world, especially in marketing and management. At the end of this study we will see how the economic sector uses the model with an example from the food industry.

Definition of the model

The pyramid of needs, also called Maslow's pyramid, offers a model for defining the needs of human beings, from the most basic functions (eating, sleeping, etc.) to the more fulfilling (self-improvement, practicing art or sports, etc.). Maslow was a psychologist, but his model, summarised by a pyramid, has been used in economics and the world of business. It offers a simple and effective way of identifying different needs, as long as they are considered as a whole, not as successive stages.

THEORY

Microeconomics naturally concerns the conditions that lead to market exchange. Maslow's pyramid is positioned ahead of these conclusions, right at the origin of the demand: needs.

THE FIVE LEVELS OF NEEDS

Level by level, Maslow brings together various human needs. He does not directly mention a pyramid form, but a hierarchy of importance: as soon as a family is satisfied, other needs appear immediately. As Maslow's hierarchy of needs covers multiple areas, including personal development, it is useful to employ the terms used by the author himself in order to understand the essence of the concept.

Maslow's Hierarchy of Needs

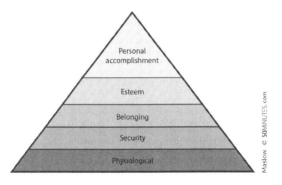

- The first level is that of **physiological needs**. Eating, drinking, sleeping, breathing, etc., are all functions related to individual survival. Since these are basic, vital needs, they are obviously the most important: they certainly exceed needs for security, esteem, etc.
- Next, **safety needs**. You might think immediately of physical integrity, but this category is not restricted to that – protection against theft and damage also fall under this category. Maslow states that safety needs lead people to prefer what is familiar, rather than the unknown.
- When these two types of needs are met, those related to love, affection or social relations (the **need to belong**) appear. This third category takes into account the social nature of the human being.
- This leads to the fourth level of the pyramid, which is the **need for esteem or recognition**. This category refers to the needs relating to status, employment, power and money that define us in society.
- Finally, at the top of the pyramid stands the **need for personal accomplishment**. While the needs of the lower levels depend on the perceptions of others, the needs at the top of the pyramid are related to the development of the individual's personality. According to Maslow, these needs can take any form, as long as they match the individual desires of the person. In other words, if I want to be a doctor, for example, a need related to becoming a doctor, such as the need to know how the human body works, appears automatically.

In Maslow's theory, you should satisfy the needs of each level, before moving up to the next one. Would someone fear for the safety of their belongings if they had nothing to eat? Would someone care about their social connections while being attacked by a group of looters? What good is recognition from others without being integrated into a social group? And how accomplished can someone feel without good self-esteem? This is therefore a dynamic model, not a strictly hierarchical presentation.

Maslow puts individual development into perspective, assuming that individuals always seek a good quality of life. In reality, needs are not the same for everyone and they also vary over time. Moreover, other types of needs may emerge with varying importance according to the people and the circumstances and coexist alongside those represented in the pyramid.

NEEDS: FROM ECONOMICS TO MARKETING

Compared to the many needs related to social relationships and humans, the need for available goods appears to be very limited. However, economic reasoning is more interested in the utility – i.e. the function of an additional unit of a product for the consumer – than the need, without prioritising the goods themselves.

The analysis of needs is more concerned with marketing and management. Needs are mostly studied at the level of the company and its market positioning. Psychologists do agree that existential and basic needs are relatively limited, but there is always a need –seen as a lack or a desire – for the product by the consumer.

Marketers are aware of this and constantly refer to Maslow's famous pyramid. Putting a product or service into the pyramid leads us to consider and develop launch strategies that are sometimes very varied. For example, we wouldn't market a staple product as a piece of high technology. It is also possible for a product or service to satisfy different levels of needs; it is then necessary to adapt the message according to the target consumers.

LIMITATIONS AND EXTENSIONS

LIMITATIONS AND CRITICISMS

Like all classic theories in social sciences, the pyramid of needs has been the subject of critical interpretation. Several weaknesses of the model are highlighted, although some are contradictory:

- **The lack of nuance in the hierarchy of needs.** Some natural functions are more important than others. You can go without eating for several days, but you can only stop breathing for a few minutes.
- **The questionable hierarchy.** It does not consider the fact that humans are social beings. Can the need to eat really be put above maintaining human relationships or self-improvement? Without food, a person cannot survive. Without sufficient interaction with others, a person's mental state will deteriorate, driving them to madness or even suicide.
- **The ethnocentrism of the model.** All studies were conducted on Western populations, resulting in an approach that only applies to wealthy, developed civilizations.

With the exception of this last point, the criticisms linked to the lack or excess of hierarchy actually refer more to the uses developed for Maslow's theory than to the theory itself. In fact, the pyramid form does not appear in Maslow's work and it hides the dynamic movement that he envisaged between the various needs.

The marginal use in public services

The use of Maslow's pyramid in economics remains fairly limited. It is impossible to analyse the definition of prices depending on the level of need. The application relates more to the marginal utility of a good (as demonstrated by the economists Léon Walras (1834-1910), William Stanley Jevons (1835-1882) and Carl Menger (1840-1921) in the 19th century), which is the satisfaction provided by an additional unit, rather than its level in Maslow's pyramid.

Remember that Maslow's pyramid is not a classification of all the needs and desires of economic agents, but a five-step model of human fulfilment. When examined in this way, this pyramid can serve as a support for the interventions of public actors in the economy: regulating food production and protecting the air quality (physiological needs), enforcing law and order (safety needs), ensuring the socialisation of children, particularly at school (love and belonging), etc. It is more difficult to consider a response to the top two levels of the pyramid. Public broadcasting, higher education and investment in culture can perhaps be understood as collective responses to the needs for self-fulfilment and recognition from others.

RELATED MODELS AND EXTENSIONS

Henderson's theory of needs

Other models have been proposed, including the model devised by Virginia Henderson (American nurse, 1897-1996), which identifies 14 needs presented in a grid. This model is widely used in the medical world. Nevertheless, the additional contribution of this model is not clear. All the categories identified fall into the five major categories of Maslow's pyramid. Also, if the limits of this model are immediately apparent, it is difficult to justify this new classification.

ERG theory

In 1969, the American psychologist Clayton Alderfer (born in 1940) presented the ERG theory (Existence, Relatedness and Growth), which is actually a more concise version of Maslow's pyramid. Instead of five levels, the ERG theory identifies three: existence needs (food, clothing, security, etc.), relatedness needs (being linked to other individuals) and growth needs (development, creativity, sense of life, self-esteem, etc.). Alderfer did not set out to reshape the categories of Maslow. For him, an individual must meet these needs simultaneously, not one after the other by climbing the levels of the pyramid. If growth needs are not satisfied, this will affect social behaviour and basic functions, like sleeping and eating. According to the psychologist, the dynamic of the needs is more comprehensive than in Maslow's model. His model has been especially successful in the fields of management and work psychology.

PRACTICAL APPLICATION

As we have seen, Maslow's pyramid has its most concrete economic application in marketing. It is not surprising that more and more models from psychology are being used for marketing purposes, as the concept of marketing is based on understanding and anticipating consumer behaviour.

PRODUCTS AND NEEDS

Rather than sticking to the categorisation of each product or service in a level of the pyramid, it is better to look at which operation can meet the most needs.

A product, a need

The most basic application is identifying the level of the pyramid where the product or service that you want to market sits: food and basic hygiene belong on the bottom level, cultural products at the top. This classification seems extremely rudimentary, but it makes sense. The organisation of supermarket shelves shows this, as its products are categorised according to their type and use.

The most basic products are often part of this process. This is especially true for staple foods. Packets of pasta or potatoes only cover the first level of the pyramid: they are designed to feed. But this strategy is rarely enough on its own. Remember that Maslow's pyramid is dynamic, and a good product or service launch must meet the maximum number of needs.

Marketing with the pyramid

Developing an offer for consumers is all to do with targeting all levels of the pyramid.

To fully understand this theory, you should define the needs in their contemporary context. New functions – which did not exist In Maslow's time (20th century) – have emerged in society. For example, if somebody moved house in the 1950s, they would not go as quickly or as far as we can today: families were closer together, and their home was usually next to their workplace. Aside from leisure purposes, the need to travel can be considered a physiological need, as it allows someone to earn a living by going to work or maintain their emotional relationships by visiting friends and relatives.

The car is an excellent example of a strategy that evolves within the pyramid. The least expensive models are limited to basic features, while the more expensive models combine prestige and comfort. In all cases, this type of product involves several levels of the pyramid: the physiological need to travel, the need to avoid the vehicles that are known for being unreliable, belonging to the community of drivers whose cars are from one particular, well-known brand, and (for the most advanced models) the satisfaction of owning an expensive, luxury good.

Marketing therefore tries to establish a strategy to meet the higher levels of the pyramid with products that seem to mainly meet the first level of needs. It also provides an opposite function, although this is more difficult. When a product or service is intended for self-esteem or personality development, a brand can focus on and emphasise the physiological and safety aspects of purchasing in order to attract the greatest number of consumers to buy the product. Think about cosmetics, where branding switches between radiant beauty (fourth and fifth levels) and self-care, maintaining the skin and body, which refers to the physiological and safety needs.

Marketing and the need for love and belonging

What about the third level of the pyramid? It seems ridiculous to imagine products that could meet the need for love. Maslow puts into this category the bonds of friendship or love, which are hard to satisfy in the market (although the success of dating sites shows that there is a place for intermediaries in the matter), as well as the membership of social groups.

For a long time, marketing has played on the prestige of a product to encourage the consumer to buy it. From the late 19th century, the sociologist and economist Thorstein Veblen (1857-1929) had identified a bias in the model of homo economicus.

EXTRA INFORMATION: HOMO ECONOMICUS

The concept of the economic man, homo economicus in Latin, reflects the theoretical behaviour of humans. Based on this abstract representation, theorists in different fields think of potential interactions between the human illustrated here and the concepts they develop.

Of course, we maximise the utility of what we buy, but imitation and even snobbery are not absent from our decisions. This analysis is an extension of the concept developed by the French sociologist Pierre Bourdieu (1930-2002): our social practices, and therefore our purchases, often respond to the desire to stand out from our peers by imitating the practices of higher social classes. By purchasing a product (a car, perfume, etc.) a consumer can also satisfy their need for social recognition.

While this is not a new trend, it has particular strength when developing multiple identities and community ties, which are supported, if not initiated, by information and communication technology, particularly social networks. Some brands play perfectly on the sense of belonging linked to simply owning the product. Think how Apple has created a user community since the 1980s: starting with the microcosm of graphic designers and image professionals, this community, which many users consider themselves to be members of, has grown exponentially thanks to the mass market and the marketing of its flagship products (iPhone, iPad, etc.). Facebook, Twitter and all social networks are also using this strategy and build on the sense of belonging, which, in this case, is at the heart of their business model, with the advantage of free advertising-related funding.

CASE STUDY – THE FOOD INDUSTRY

Finally, let's look in more detail at an economic sector: the food industry. This sector has been particularly well designed to satisfy all levels of the pyramid and to continue developing more innovative products.

The food industry: a five-stage economy

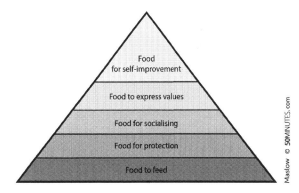

Food
for self-improvement

Food to express values

Food for socialising

Food for protection

Food to feed

Maslow © **50**MINUTES.com

Food to feed

Of course, the food industry meets a physiological need: the need to eat. There is no need to dwell on this aspect, except to emphasise how the value of an industrial sector remains limited if it only responds to one strict need. In order to grow, the value chain has also incorporated many different purposes, other than just satisfying hunger.

Food for protection

The food industry is built on safety as well. Due to the regulations that govern the manufacturing of products, the industry is obliged to offer more certified food than the old artisan producers (however, it should be pointed out that this argument was valid at the time of development but now artisanal products are also subject to strict hygiene standards). At one time, home canning exposed many families to the risk of botulism (a type of food poisoning with serious consequences), which was not a danger with industrial canning.

Today, a second level of security has been added, since manufacturers have invested in the niche of 'functional foods', also known as nutraceuticals. Cholesterol-lowering margarine, fortified milk (which encourages growth in children), grains that help digestion or mineral water that strengthens the immune system have all thrived in supermarkets. Their health claims are also more and more strictly monitored.

Food for socialising

Food, especially in the Western world, is deeply embedded in our culture. A meal is a source of conviviality and a time for sharing. Industrial suppliers have naturally seized the opportunity to offer products that meet this need for belonging and social ties. Here are three examples that fall into this category:

- 'traditional' ready meals that claim to revive traditions and bring the consumer closer to the culinary identity of their country;

- festive and innovative products as snacks or desserts that create a certain amount of conviviality;
- large brands with different products for different target markets, especially those with products based around childhood, that cross generations and focus on the taste of foods being a shared identity among everyone that consumes them, creating continuity between parents and children (Nutella, Haribo, Kinder, Banania, etc.).

The development of halal, kosher and Asian departments in supermarkets also matches the identity side of food, helping immigrant populations to maintain a link with their native culture through their food purchases.

Food to express values

More recently, the food industry has addressed the issue of values, this time not necessarily in an economic sense. After the simultaneous appearance of major retail chains and the industrialisation of food, there were a lot of questions to answer. Concern about GMOs, the mad cow disease crisis of the 1990s followed by the Beef Hormone Dispute, successive campaigns on obesity and excess sugar in our foods have led consumers to want further explanations. Environmental awareness and the search for distinctive differentiations in a globalised world have reinforced this expectation.

It is this need for belonging and value that resulted in labels, names and other guidelines that have spread through the food sector. 'Organic farming', 'fair trade' and 'regional products' have become labels that we constantly see on the shelves. They provide information about the quality or origin of the food, along with information about the production conditions. The fields are very broad: compensation of local workers, not using pesticides, respecting ancient culinary traditions, etc. Everyone is free to choose their preferred products, as long as the label matches their values.

Food for personal development

Finally, food – and therefore the food industry – also reflects the top level of the pyramid, namely self-realisation and personal fulfilment.

High-end products, such as great vintage wines, artisanal coffee, fine chocolate or rare teas, delight consumers beyond the simple need to satisfy hunger or thirst. Gastronomy, if not an art, is surely a craft of excellence that meets a consumer's need for accomplishment. This is certainly embodied by great chefs or bakers, but it also has an outlet in the food industry.

Offering consumers the simple possibility of undertaking part of the recipe themselves can also satisfy the need for accomplishment. This is why the industry provides kits for making pancakes or cakes, and also offers many pre-prepared products to help with cooking 'home-made dishes', allowing consumers to help to make it, and therefore giving them the opportunity to express their creativity.

SUMMARY

- The pyramid of needs offers a model of five levels that categorise human needs.
- This dynamic model details the five sequential steps necessary for human development: physiological needs, a sense of security, recognition, self-esteem and accomplishment.
- Theorised by American psychologist Abraham Maslow, it was rarely used in economics because it says nothing about the concrete development of demand, i.e. turning a customer desire into a purchase.
- Although its simplicity has been criticised, it is still a strong point of the model. The pyramid is widely used in marketing, as positioning a product or service in the pyramid, while trying, if possible, to meet needs on several levels, leads to developing a relevant strategy.

We want to hear from you!
Leave a comment on your online library
and share your favourite books on social media!

FURTHER READING

BIBLIOGRAPHY

- Bouchiki, H., Cerdin, J-L., Dornier, P-P., Esnault, B., Le Nagard-Assayag, E. and Mottis, N. (2001) *Invitation au management*. Paris: Presses universitaires de France.
- Fenouillet, F. (No date) Modèle hiérarchique des besoins. *La motivation, un concept puzzle*. [Online]. [Accessed 5 May 2014]. Available from: <http://www.lesmotiva-tions.net/spip.php?article40>
- Jacquemin, A., Tulkens, H. and Mercier, P. (2000) *Fondements d'économie politique*. [3rd edition]. Brussels: Boeck University.
- Lambin, J.-J. and Moerloose, C. (2012) *Marketing stratégique et opérationnel*. [8th edition]. Paris: DUNOD.
- Maslow, A. (2003) *Devenir le meilleur de soi-même : besoins fondamentaux, motivations et personnalité*. Paris: Eyrolles.
- Mias, L. (No date) Maslow, Henderson, soins. *Papidoc*. [Online]. [Accessed 5 May 2014]. Available from: <http://papidoc.chic-cm.fr/573MaslowBesoins.html>

Printed in Great Britain
by Amazon